Bestselling books by Heather Baker

Speed Writing
Dictionary
ISBN: 978-1534683204

How to Take Minutes
of Meetings
ISBN: 978-1532737602

Successful Business
Writing
ISBN: 978-1532737688

Bestselling books from UoLearn

How to Write
Excellent Reports
ISBN: 978-1849370899

Developing Your
Assertiveness
ISBN: 978-1537637723

Developing Your
Influencing Skills
ISBN: 978-1537637785

Order books from Amazon or your favourite
bookseller and from www.uolearn.com

The exceptional PA - move from good to great

For personal assistants, executive assistants and office professionals to help develop excellent emotional intelligence, management skills and interpersonal skills to excel at work. Build excellent relationships through confidence and assertiveness to become the best you can be.

Published by: Universe of Learning Ltd,
reg number 6485477, Lancashire, UK
www.UoLearn.com, support@UoLearn.com

ISBN 978-1-84937-095-0

Contents

About the author

Heather had over twenty years' experience as a secretary and PA before setting up Baker Thompson Associates Limited in 2000. The company specialises in the training and development of PA and administrative staff, www.bakerthompsonassoc.co.uk.

She now travels all over the world working with large and small companies to enable their office staff and PAs to work more effectively and efficiently. She is an acclaimed international speaker and has worked in a wide variety of places including London, Liverpool, Paris, Abu Dhabi, Dubai, Singapore, Washington DC, Shanghai, Melbourne, Sydney and Johannesburg. She is a bestselling author of books on speed writing, minute taking and business writing. She is the creator of the Bakerwrite speed writing system that is used all over the world.

She worked for ICI Pharmaceuticals (now AstraZeneca) and Hewlett Packard; she spent five years in France working for the Commercial Director of Cognac Hine and then 10 years with Granada Media working up to Personal Assistant to the Managing Director, commuting regularly between their offices in Manchester and London.

She wrote this book to help other administrators move from good to exceptional sharing her experience of being a high-level PA.

Heather has been married to Ian since 1979 and they have two daughters, Ailsa and Erin. This book is dedicated to them with profound thanks for all their support over the years.

The Exceptional PA

Who are you and what do you want?

Are you a PA, an aspiring PA or an EA? Are you a secretary, administrator, office manager or any of the other 600 plus titles for office professionals? Approximately one-fifth of the world's working population are in similar roles.

The perceptions of the role are not always very positive and members of the profession can feel used and abused. What would you like? Some ideas might be: respect, success, less stress, a career path, training opportunities, support or excellent relationships with colleagues and managers?

How would you know if you had this? Feeling less negatively stressed, receiving praise, being included, treated as an equal, offered opportunities, creating opportunities, improved work environment, success?

How could you achieve this? Things you could use are learning, training, sharing good practice, networking, reading, discussions or emotional intelligence.

This book will set you on the path for the success you would like. It will give you an extended insight into the vital basics of communications, confidence and assertiveness. It will continue to develop your skills using neuro-linguistic programming techniques, reflecting on leadership, emotional intelligence, management and goal setting.

Introduction

I have been wanting to write a book for PAs for many years but always felt it was just such a wide subject that I couldn't do it justice.

I finally made the decision to take a particular focus.

There are now quite a few very good books for PAs available. Many of them include topics such as diary management, organising your time and your manager's time and much more. My own books, already published, focus on minute taking, BakerWrite speedwriting and business writing.

For this book I'm going to assume my readers already work as effective PAs and are capable of managing their manager's diary, travel, etc. You are already successfully organising events, attending meetings and possibly giving presentations.

In this book I want to focus on the "added extra" skills that a top flight PA needs and look at these in more depth, and, not in a general way, but particularly in relation to their role.

When I was working for the MD of Granada, we tried to find bespoke PA training for someone at my level, offering the extra skills that I needed to work in my role. At that time, in the mid-1990s, there was nobody doing this (at least not in the UK). Oh yes, there were PA courses, but these were often fairly low level and facilitated by people who had never even worked in the role. I eventually attended a management course, which was extremely useful, but, nevertheless, not totally focussed on my type of role. Nobody was helping office professionals step up; nobody was empowering them...

It was at this time that the seed of an idea came to me: someone, who has actually been a PA, should be offering training to PAs. In 2000 an opportunity arose for me to take redundancy from Granada when my manager needed to be based in London (we spent most of the week there already). I wanted to stay based in Manchester and that is when I took all the steps needed to start Baker Thompson Associates (www. bakerthompsonassoc.co.uk).

Since then, I have worked with many varied organisations, public and private, in the UK and around the world, to help OPs (office professionals) excel in their roles and thus enable the success of their company... and it has been a delight.

I have had opportunities to meet PAs from multi-nationals, small family businesses, banks, universities, football clubs, media organisations, gold and oil businesses and so much more. I have written articles for PA magazines and blogs and I regularly present at PA seminars and conferences.

Since I started training in January 2000 the PA world has "exploded"; the roles are finally getting the respect they deserve and PAs have become a highly targeted market by so many different companies who understand their decision making powers.

What a different world from when I tried to find a relevant course. You can now learn about the role from websites, social media and webinars, as well as from training courses.

I hear people suggest that the role of the PA is no longer relevant.

"Does that role still exist?" I was asked when I explained what I do. "I thought nobody needed PAs anymore...".

After I'd metaphorically picked myself up from the floor, I said "Yes, very much so".

Technological innovations and changes in working practice have considerably altered the role of the PA, but it is a continually invaluable role and a truly effective manager will always need a PA.

The secretarial role, now usually referred to as administrative, has also changed. Whereas 40 years ago every manager would have a secretary, even if occasionally shared, nowadays it is more common for organisations to have a pool of administrators working for a large number of executives. Funnily enough, about 10 years ago, I worked with some former typists from a pool whom their organisation had decided should become secretaries to the various groups. This was a big step forward for what was an old family business. Are we now going back the other way?

The PA role, however, involves so much more. The modern PA (or EA) has a management role. He or she (because many more men are now taking up these important positions) is very much involved in the business. It is no longer purely a task based role and is increasingly about building relationships.

The modern PA will have all the basic skills of shorthand or speedwriting, IT and organisational skills and they will also be fully business aware through attending meetings, networking and research.

They will be experts in building relationships, dealing with conflict and decision making. They are emotionally intelligent leaders, who are prepared to take risks and be creative. They must be willing to represent their manager, give presentations and attend meetings and delegate.

Their main personal qualities are loyalty, reliability, flexibility and, of course, that vital sense of fun.

Most importantly they are committed to their manager, their organisation and their own development. They are prepared to invest time in training, being proactive, collaborating and grasping opportunities. An exceptional PA does not believe in luck; he/she makes their own luck.

This is what this book aims to help you do:

- ✓ Understand how we communicate
- ✓ Exude confidence
- ✓ Use assertiveness to gain respect
- ✓ Understand NLP techniques to build relationships and create excellence
- ✓ Manage staff successfully
- ✓ Be a leader
- ✓ Make decisions under pressure
- ✓ Gain business acumen
- ✓ Network successfully
- ✓ Ensure positive perceptions
- ✓ Emotional intelligence
- ✓ Set clear and viable goals

This book starts with the basic explanations of communications, confidence and assertiveness and develops to more advanced aspects as it progresses. Some of the topics overlap.

Glossary of terms

EA   Executive Assistant

EI   Emotional intelligence

NLP   Neuro-linguistic programming

OP   Office Professional

PA   Personal Assistant

Chapter 1:
Understand how we communicate

"Communication - the human connection - is the key to personal and career success."
Paul J. Meyer

Chapter 1
Understand how
we communicate

In this chapter we look at:

• Communication

• Body language

• Listening and talking

We can't NOT communicate; we all do it all day every day in work and outside of work. I have a fun activity I do with people on courses where they are not allowed to communicate; I can't tell you how many people find it virtually impossible – with great hilarity, of course!

We have been communicating since we were born and, as we get older, our skills become more refined – in most cases.

How we communicate depends on so many things, starting with how our parents or guardians communicated with us (I'll reflect on this in the chapter on emotional intelligence). It is sad to see adults who shout aggressively or who interrupt and have no consideration for the person they are speaking with. This is usually because that is what happened to them as they were growing up.

As parents, adults in general, we must instil an understanding of heightened communication skills.

It is fairly common knowledge that we communicate with others in three main ways; through our words, our tone of voice and our body language. What can surprise people is that the majority of the messages we give to others are through our body language (over 50%). Secondly our tone of voice is vital and, in fact, words are only about 7% of how people pick up messages from us.

If our body language and tone of voice don't back up our words, then nobody will believe us. We try to say things to avoid conflict but, if we are gritting our teeth and standing with our hands on our hips, it totally ruins the impact of our words and results in more conflict.

A few times delegates have said to me, "I wasn't aggressive, I just told him, 'look'" and this while holding their hand up in front of them.

I don't know about you, but I would immediately feel threatened.

Body Language

Let's look at body language first as that is the most important aspect of getting across messages.

Some examples of threatening or aggressive body language could be:

- ✗ Hands on hips
- ✗ Leaning too close into someone
- ✗ Staring at people
- ✗ Waving fists
- ✗ Putting a hand up to a person
- ✗ Pointing
- ✗ Frowning
- ✗ Talking through gritted teeth
- ✗ Scowling
- ✗ Turning our back on somebody

Now, here are signs of passivity through body language:

- ✗ Hanging head
- ✗ Drooping shoulders
- ✗ Frowning
- ✗ Not making eye contact
- ✗ Fiddling with hair or hands
- ✗ Fidgeting
- ✗ Biting lip
- ✗ Covering face (particularly mouth) with hands

These are ways we can emit positive, assertive signs:

- ✓ Stand straight
- ✓ Shoulders back
- ✓ Smile
- ✓ Make good eye contact
- ✓ Open arms
- ✓ Friendly hand gestures

**** Exercise ****

Give examples of body language you have seen other people use. What was the message you received from it?

Are you aware of your own body language? What messages do you think you might be inadvertently transmitting?

....

....

....

....

****

With all these examples, take care not to assume that someone is being aggressive because they are frowning; they may just be concentrating. Usually it is a mixture of signs that indicate definite aggression, passivity or assertiveness.

These basics of communication are vital to an effective PA as you are both reading other people and ensuring you are giving out the right message to colleagues, managers and clients.

Your manager wants to feel confident that you know what you are doing. Reinforce that confidence by adopting assertive body language.

Body language that show passivity and a lack of confidence:

What we should be doing:

**** Exercise ****

Stand in front of a mirror and practise assertive body language. When you're watching TV or videos try to label the type of body language you see. Soaps are particularly good for this as they often exaggerate the body language.

Notes:

....

....

....

....

....

****

Listening and talking

In the 21st century the role of the PA is very much relationship based. The best PAs engender respect and admiration from colleagues and managers and this is done through leadership which is based on excellent communication. An emotionally intelligent PA will not only give out confident signals, he or she will also be very aware of other people's body language to ensure they fully understand what a person is trying to get across. Don't just listen; listen and observe.

**** Exercise ****

Sit down with another person so that you are facing each other and ask them to talk to you for 2 minutes (about work, a holiday, something that made them angry, anything they like etc.). Listen to them, without talking, but, most importantly, watch them; note down all the visuals you notice – eye movements, body positions, skin colour changes, expressions, etc. Don't write down your interpretation of what you see; just what you see. For example, don't write "she looked cross", write "she was scowling". Compare how the physical matched the story they were telling.

....

....

....

....

....

****

We can take this a step further and be aware of eye movements. In the majority of cases, eyes going up to the left shows the speaker is constructing an image and, therefore, potentially lying. Eyes going up the right mean they are remembering and, therefore, probably telling the truth.

Visual
Constructed

Visual
Remembered

Auditory
Constructed

Auditory
Remembered

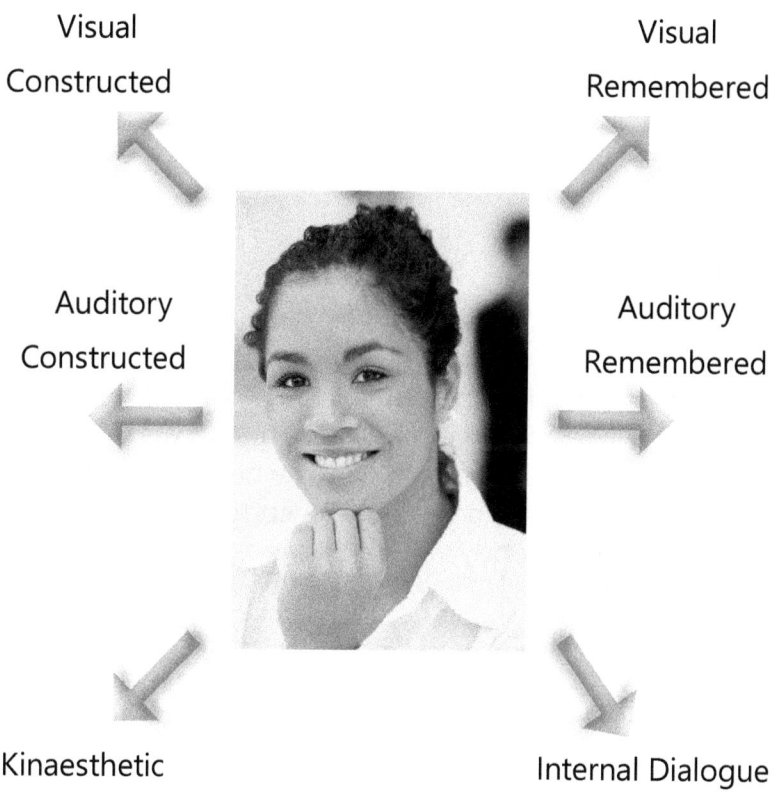

Kinaesthetic

Internal Dialogue

Ask someone to tell you what pink snow looks like and see which way their eyes move. As they have probably never seen this, they will have to construct an image. Next ask them to describe their front door. The eyes should go to the right as they will be remembering.

******

The next aspect is the tone of voice. Think of how many ways you can say "I'm fine"; happily, sarcastically, wearily, and so on. It's very good to use the best words when communicating with people, but if you are not using the correct tone, again, as with body language, nobody will be convinced.

**** Exercise ****

Take a simple phrase such as thank you and see how many ways you can say it.

******

When communicating with your manager, or colleagues or clients, think about the tone of voice you are using as well as the words.

**** **Exercise** ****

What may make your tone of voice inappropriate?

[Suggestions for some of the exercises can be found at the back of the book.]

....

....

....

....

....

****

When people are preparing for interviews, they often tell me they are very well prepared because they've anticipated plenty of questions and have answers prepared and have also thought of questions to ask. Have they, though, thought about their tone of voice when speaking in the interview – and their body language too? It's all part of the planning; theoretically, the most important part.

It's not just interviews though; it's also preparing for attending meetings, giving presentations, delegating to colleagues and, very importantly, resolving conflict.

Assertiveness of tone is through good volume (not too loud, not whispering) and good modulation. Modulation is making your voice sound friendly, confident and not monotonous. You should vary the pitch, but not too much and never speak too quickly.

When you are on the telephone particularly (where you have no visuals), it is good just to deliver short phrases rather than giving a lot of information like machine gun fire!

Compare these:

1. "Good morning. My name's Heather Baker and I'm phoning about the stand at the next PA Show because I'd like to arrange for some electricity so that we can have some lights on the exhibits."

2. "Good morning. My name's Heather Baker."

   "Good morning, Heather. How may I help you?"

"I'm calling about my stand at the PA Show."

   "OK, what can we do for you?"

"I wanted to discuss having electricity to the stand for some lighting." ......

Number 2 is calmer, more elegant and less stressful for the person taking the call. You, the PA, come across as someone in control, confident and aware of your position, knowledge and experience.

**** Exercise ****

Think of how you could break down your delivery for calls that you have to make.

Notes:

....

....

....

....

....

****

It reinforces the positive perceptions you want to give; we will come back to this in detail later in this book.

Let us now consider the words we use, although not as easy to "read" as body language and tone of voice, our words are nevertheless incredibly important in our communication.

It is, unfortunately, extremely easy to make a statement sarcastic, aggressive or passive, despite assertive body language and tone, by the use of certain words – in the wrong way.

Take these phrases:

"I was just saying" or "I was only saying".

These can come across as aggressive in certain situations and could ruin a good attempt at being assertive.

Here are some other examples:

"If you'd have done that in the first place."

"Can you just...."

"No, that's not right."

I'm sure you can think of many more.

By just rephrasing slightly, our message can be so much more positive:

"What I was hoping to say was...."

"Let's look at how we can make sure this doesn't happen again."

"That's one thought; could I make another suggestion too?"

I'm using much more inclusive words – "we" instead of "you"; this becomes less accusing. Use questions rather than statements to show that you are considering the other person's thoughts.

**** Exercise ****

Think of examples of aggressive words and phrases you may have heard.

Notes:

....

....

....

....

....

******

What we are trying to do is not "trash" other people's ideas. I remember a rather aggressive delegate telling me that I never told anyone they were wrong. "How can I," I replied, "when I am asking them how they feel?"

A huge part of emotional intelligence is remembering that everyone has a different story.

Chapter 2
Develop your Confidence

"Believe in yourself! Have faith in your abilities!
Without a humble but reasonable confidence in
your own powers you cannot be successful or happy."
Norman Vincent Peale

Chapter 2
Develop your Confidence

In this chapter we look at:

- Positive attitude
- Concentrate on your strengths
- Know your subject
- Body language
- Plan a strategy
- Don't apologise
- Dress appropriately

If an excellent understanding of communication skills is the most important ability of an administrator, then confidence and assertiveness are next in line.

On all my PA courses we start with communications, which then gives us the basics to continue with confidence and assertiveness. We then have all the tools we need for every other aspect of an effective PA's "collection".

It's not always **being** confident that is important, it is **appearing** confident that matters more.

Most days as a PA I had times when I was less confident in what I was doing or saying, even after many years' experience. What I learnt was that no matter how concerned I felt, I should rarely let it show. I have to say, though, that the more confident

I acted, the more confident I actually became.

"Fake it till you make it!"

Here are some ways to be (or at least appear) more confident:

Positive attitude:

If we always assume that things will go wrong, why would we be confident? NLP (Neuro-linguistic programming – more later) teaches us about reframing, that is seeing the glass half full rather than half empty (or drinking the water to solve the problem!).

Make a determined effort to see negatives as positives. Find a reason why the problem could be a solution. My former Chief Executive used to say, "There are no such things as problems, only challenges".

**** Exercise ****

Why do you think people see the negative side of things? Remember this is not just about you, it's also about your understanding of other people (emotional intelligence).

Notes:

....

....

....

....

....

****

It's not about being unrealistic, it's about finding some good, some positives in everything. When this attitude becomes your normal state, you will always feel more confident as you don't expect the worst.

If your manager is a negative person, counteract the negativity with positive options. More positivity in relationships in business leads to more effective partnerships.

Moreover, negative people are extremely unattractive. In general, we all want to be with people who are positive. Your positivity will attract people to your circle so you will gain respect. This, in turn, will make you feel more confident and enable you to be a truly effective PA. It is a virtuous circle.

**** Exercise ****

Change these negative phrases into more positive statements.

1. "I'm having a terrible day."

2. "That's going to be really difficult."

3. "Why do they have to keep changing things?"

Notes:

....

....

....

....

....

****

Concentrate on your strengths:

Most of us, as we travel home from work, reflect on the mistakes we may have made during the day. That is not a bad thing, however, don't forget to reflect on the things that went well too.

We so often let the errors, mistakes and misunderstandings take priority in our thoughts over the positives. It is good to consider our mistakes:

* Why did I do it?

* How can I make sure it doesn't happen again?

Then move on. Consider the successes of your day; no matter how small. This is giving yourself a pat on the back – in case nobody else does!

It also helps to boost your self-confidence and ensure you don't let one or two small mistakes cause you to perform less well in future.

Case study

Jane, a senior PA, drove home feeling very low. She had failed to correctly assess the importance of a decision to be made. Based on her knowledge and wide experience, she had decided it was not urgent to contact one of her director's managers to keep him up to date. However, she had failed to realise that the event also impacted on another project he was working on, in which Jane was less involved.

Once she realised, it was obvious and she was very angry with herself. She had had to make the decision very quickly as she was also involved in arranging an urgent meeting for her manager. This meeting went ahead and, as a result of her rapid response, the company obtained a large new order.

A normal day in the life of a PA but why do we also focus on the negatives. Keep a good balance.

Sometimes we also use self-deprecation to avoid seeming pompous or "above ourselves". Modesty is good but so too is being aware of our skills and talents.

If you have particular abilities, make sure people know so that your skills can be put to the best use. If somebody thanks you for doing a good job, don't say "oh, it was nothing". Say "thank you". It is imperative that OPs share their knowledge with each other; this is incredibly empowering.

If somebody compliments you on your clothes or your appearance and you deny the compliment, it could be compared to being given a present and throwing it on the floor... Say "thank you".

Finally, don't consider yourself a lesser person because you don't have the same qualifications or skills as another. You have your own qualities and training and, coupled with your emotional intelligence and organisational skills, you can be so valuable to yourself and others. Everyone in an organisation is there to enable the success of that organisation. It shouldn't matter how much someone earns or what their position is; everyone is valuable.

Bullying is completely unacceptable in any organisation and, in fact, can be a factor in a company's lack of success. We will look at this topic later.

**** Exercise ****

What are the special skills and/or qualities that you bring to your role? How do these complement your manager's skills and qualities?

....

....

....

....

....

****

Know your subject:

The first week in a new job seems like a year! This is because everything is unfamiliar, we often don't know anyone properly and we are very much out of our comfort zone. We start to feel more confident over the ensuing weeks as we understand and familiarise ourselves with topics and colleagues.

It is the same in any situation; the less we know the less confidence we will have. Instead of worrying about this, we should be doing something about it.

Before putting ourselves in any situation where we are going to feel nervous and lacking confidence, we should prepare as much as possible. We do it for interviews as we discussed earlier. We should do similar preparation for all situations we encounter. It might be for meetings, networking events, presentations, negotiations and even our daily chat with the manager.

To prepare ourselves we should get as much information as possible. Business acumen is vital to a strategic, confident and effective PA. Here are some things you could do:

✓ Talk to people who are experts in a related field

✓ Research via the internet or organisations' intranets

✓ Read emails, documents, reports, minutes

✓ Keep an eye on notice boards

✓ Listen to what people are saying

✓ Keep up to date with media – TV, radio, newspapers (paper or online) and trade magazines

✓ Learn about people's roles and preferences – remember their names

What could you personally do to really gain business acumen for your organisation?

....

....

....

....

....

****

Before going into meetings with your manager, make sure you are prepared and have any relevant information with you. Then, anticipate any questions he/she may have and ensure you can offer viable solutions.

Body language:

We discussed body language in Chapter 1 and learnt how it is the main way that people interpret our behaviour and how we understand others.

If we wish to appear confident, having confident body language is paramount. Assuming a confident body stance can actually make a person feel more confident. For example, if you have a tricky 'phone call to make; stand up. The person you are calling can't see you so it doesn't matter. Try and avoid aggressive pacing though as that will reflect in your tone of voice.

In the chapter on networking, we will reflect further on what to do to ensure confident body language. However, in the meantime you might like to watch social psychologist Amy Cuddy's TED talk at http://www.ted.com/talks/amy_cuddy_your_body_language_shapes_who_you_are?language=en.

Plan a strategy – mental rehearsal

You have a meeting with your manager (or a colleague or client), it's a delicate subject and you are very worried about how it will go. Rather than worrying, do some constructive preparation. Here is a checklist for you:

1. Decide the objective of your meeting

2. Decide what you are prepared to accept and what would be unacceptable

3. Consider what would be the best time for the conversation

4. Research the topic, read the background, ensure you are fully briefed

5. What will you wear?

6. Where will the meeting take place? What are the seating arrangements – where do you want to sit?

7. Will your manager start the discussion or are you going to open the debate?

8. What might your manager say? And how would you reply?

9. How would you open the conversation? How do you think your manager might reply?

10. In both 8 & 9 above, consider what you might say if your manager says something you hadn't thought of. This might be "Could I have some time to think about that?"or "I didn't have that information; could I come back to you?". Always try and avoid saying "I don't know". It is an extremely negative phrase and can engender a negative reaction from managers. It would be much more effective to say, "Leave it with me; let me find out for you".

11. Remember that it's OK not to know everything, but a positive response creates a much more positive perception of you.

12. You can choose how you react so react confidently. (We'll talk more about this later.)

Use this checklist next time you have to prepare for a tricky meeting.

Don't apologise

I'm not saying don't ever apologise, but beware of constantly apologising, particularly for things that are not your fault.

If you have made a mistake, apologise – once. Repeated sorries can be very irritating to an aggressive person and give a perception of you as a passive, not assertive, person.

You can say you are sorry to hear that something has happened but don't take responsibility for something that is out of your control.

You may have seen the advert for Pantene shampoo "Why are women always apologising?" https://www.youtube.com/watch?v=TcGKxLJ4ZGI

**** Exercise ****

Think of ways you could express these without using the word "sorry" while maintaining a caring and concerned tone:

1. Sorry I couldn't do the report by midday.

2. Sorry, could I just ask you something?

3. Sorry, could I just reach that book from behind you?

4. Sorry, do you want to sit here?

....

....

....

....

....

****

Dress appropriately

There is nothing more likely to knock your confidence than not being dressed correctly for the occasion. It's not about "power dressing", it's about feeling comfortable and appropriate.

Always consider what you are going to wear at the start of the day. Take into account the weather, your comfort, how formal or informal you should be and practicality. High heels in Guernsey cobbled streets are not recommended (as I found out)!

Consider also the colours that suit you. People should notice you and not your clothes. If you wear the wrong colours or styles, that is what people may notice.

Many people don't suit black or white. Black may make a person look slimmer, but it can drain the colour from the face of most blonde people, for example.

It's also not always about the colour, but more the shade. People can wear some shades of green or red, for example, but not others. When you buy clothes put them up to your face in a good light; if it makes you look healthy then it's right for you. If you look drained, put it back on the rail! Don't always go for colours you like; go for colours that like you.

Be assertive

So you now know how to at least seem confident and that is the first step to becoming assertive. The next chapter talks you through how to do this.

Chapter 3:

Gain respect by being assertive

"Honest communication is built on truth and integrity and upon respect of the one for the other." Benjamin E. Mays

Chapter 3
Gain respect by being assertive

In this chapter we look at :

- What is assertiveness?
- Knowledge
- Confidence
- Voice control
- State the facts
- Give yourself time
- Ask questions
- Plan ahead

What is assertiveness?

Assertiveness is the art of communicating your opinions, beliefs, feelings and wants in a direct, honest and non-aggressive way.

Assertiveness means respecting your own wishes and the wishes of others.

" ... and the wishes of others"; that's what makes the big difference between assertiveness and aggression. Being assertive means showing emotional intelligence; not being self-centred and putting yourself in another person's place.

Knowledge

Knowing your subject, understanding the people involved, planning your strategy, doing your research, preparing; all vital for you to come across as assertive. You also need to know how to react confidently when you haven't anticipated something.

Someone with a lack of knowledge will seem passive and may even cover up their ignorance by being aggressive.

Always prepare before going into any situation where you need to be assertive. For a PA this can be many times a day. Preparation may only take seconds but it is vital. Some thought before speaking, although taking a bit of time, means a PA will be truly effective and this could save time in the long run as mistakes can be avoided (see chapter 2).

It is also about considering the other person, as we mentioned earlier.

"People may forget what you say,
they may forget what you do,
but they never forget how you made them feel."
(Maya Angelou)

Make someone feel good and they are yours forever. When people are willing to help you, this saves everyone's time and reduces stress.

**** Exercise ****

Next time you have a tricky meeting, spend some time making sure you have all the background information about the topic and the person. What might you consider?

....

....

....

****

Confidence

It is pretty much impossible to be assertive if we don't feel confident.

See chapter 2.

Voice control

We've already established that tone of voice is about 40% of how we pick up messages from people (less than body language, but considerably more than words alone). It is therefore imperative that, to be perceived as an assertive PA, you have to sound like one.

Ideally you will speak clearly, not too loudly, nor too quietly. You will not speak too quickly, nor too much. Give information in small "bite-size" pieces rather than inflicting "machine gunfire" on your listener.

Never let your sentences fade away at the end; say what you have to say and then stop (more later). Make sure you are smiling, if appropriate, as this can be heard in your tone of voice.

State the facts, be honest, no emotion or exaggeration

Let me give you an example: imagine you have a work experience person in your office; a young person, say 16 years old. You ask him to type a document for you. When he has finished he gives you the document to check; it is full of spelling mistakes. You have three options:

1. Passive response: you say nothing, you don't want to upset him. This is wrong for so many reasons – he will never learn, sending out a document with spelling mistakes will reflect badly on the organisation and if you were to retype it, that would be a waste of your time.

2. Aggressive response: you speak sternly to him or shout at him, telling him that what he has done looks really bad and is not acceptable. He should go and redo it. Again, this is not a good idea. A young person will easily lose confidence by being shouted at or dealt with thoughtlessly. He may not yet have learnt about work standards. You would earn no respect as a leader and the young person would probably not want to work with you.

3. Assertive response: this is what you should do. You thank him for typing the document promptly, you point out that there are spelling mistakes and that you and he ("we" rather than "you") need to talk about the standard of letters that are sent out from the company – perhaps you will get him a dictionary. You could finish by telling him it is nicely laid out, for example.

In this way it is hoped that the young person would learn from his mistakes but not lose confidence. He may even feel appreciated that you are prepared to invest time in his development.

Remember, it's how you make people feel...

Watch out for phrases such as "I've told you thousands of times" – very aggressive and probably not true. Why not replace it with "we have spoken about this a couple of times"? And don't include that word "actually".

Assertiveness is not about avoiding the issue, it's about raising the issue in a way that doesn't result in conflict.

Aim to achieve the best solution for all concerned

The assertive PA is going to find ways to reach solutions that please the majority or are the best for the organisation, without "trashing" other people's thoughts and suggestions.

Case study

A lady on an assertiveness session I presented realised she had, unintentionally, spoken rather aggressively to her assistant. The secretary had set up a meeting room with tables and display boards. When she had finished my delegate went to have a look at the room. The first thing she said was "That table doesn't go there, it goes over there." The secretary walked out. My lady realised she had spoken aggressively but asked me what she could have said as the table was in the wrong place. First of all I asked her, "How do you know?" In her eyes it was, but in her assistant's eyes it wasn't.

I proposed saying "Thank you for setting up the room. I see you've put the table on the left, we usually put it on the right; what do you think?" There may have been a good reason that my lady hadn't thought of or the assistant might have just said "no problem"; at least she wouldn't have felt demeaned.

Don't "fill the gap"

As a young PA I often thought I had to have all the answers for my manager when he asked me a question. Consequently, when I was asked something I didn't know the answer to, I would gabble and waffle which, of course, gave the impression I was nervous, passive – frankly rather ineffective!

I soon learnt to say what I had to say and then stop talking. Often that may be: "leave it with me; I'll find out."

Also, though, when I received cold calls for my manager or had to deal with people who wanted to speak to him but I knew he didn't want to speak to them, I could become flustered and then keep talking.

It is so much better, so much more assertive to make a statement and then stop. That statement may be "I'm afraid he's not available at the moment, if you send an email we will contact you if we wish to pursue the issue."

Have a few phrases ready at your "fingertips" for any situations you may encounter.

**** Exercise ****

Prepare some phrases which you may be able to use.

....

....

....

....

....

....

....

....

****

Give yourself time

If you are asked about something and you are not sure of the answer, we have already suggested you say "leave it with me" rather than "I don't know". Continuing this theme, you may be asked for your views or thoughts about something and may not be sure. Again, don't feel you have to reply immediately if you are hesitant or unsure.

"Could I come back to you on that?" or "That's a good point, let me have a think and come back to you." These are much more assertive ways for a PA to respond to a manager.

Of course, very often OPs and managers are working at such a fast pace, this is not practical. You may want to open your reply with "my immediate response is ...."

I have had experiences when people have given negative comments to me which I felt were undeserved. Because of feeling hurt, we often become defensive, passive or aggressive and consequently less effective.

If a manager is criticising her PA, he may want to think about why he did something and explain that to her with clarity. He can give himself time by saying "at that stage I thought it was the correct thing to do"... and then stop talking.

And remember, avoid apologising if you've not done anything wrong.

Don't accuse

One of the most common ways of being aggressive is by accusing people: "you shouldn't have done that", "it was your fault that happened", "why did you say that?".

We do it sometimes because we are scared, angry or outraged. However, it will make a bad situation worse and may create problems where none existed.

Remember what we have already said; we are trying to find win-win solutions and we don't always know the other person's "story".

Avoid saying "you", rather say "we". Instead of "you did that wrong", say "can we chat about how we do this?". A PA who has been criticised by a manager for not doing something, for example, may reply "well, you never told me". This could come across as petulant and doesn't help the perceptions of you. Instead you may say "I acted on the information I had at the time". Again, try to have some assertive phrases ready for potential situations.

Avoid being passive or aggressive

It is easy to react passively or aggressively, but a top PA will always stop before speaking and acting to consider the assertive option first. And remember, it's not just what you say, it's how you say it and what you are doing at the same time – verbal, vocal and visual – the triple threat!

Ask questions

Another technique I found very effective (with teenage girls as well as managers!) was asking questions.

I once arrived at a hotel to find they did not have my booking; despite having a printed confirmation.

My situation was resolved when I asked the receptionist, "what would you do in my place?". She had more empathy for my situation and put me in an upgraded room.

You may have two managers each insisting their work has priority over the other person's. You could say to them, "which do you think is most important for the company's objectives today?" Of course, they'll probably both fight their own corner, but it could take the pressure off you and show that you are trying to help and that everyone should be pulling together for the success of the organisation.

Incidentally, the teenage girl's question is, "Are you going to tidy your room before dinner or afterwards?" Always let them think they have choices! They'll usually say "afterwards" so they can delay or potentially avoid the task!

Body language

As we have said, body language is the most telling of all the ways we communicate.

I have suggested ways you can speak to people, phrases and questions you could use, but you need to have assertive body language too, otherwise it defeats the objective.

Keep your body relaxed, non-threatening arm positioning and not frowning. Smiling may not always be appropriate, but try to keep your face fairly neutral.

If someone is speaking to you aggressively, don't let yourself become passive by rounding your shoulders, biting your nails, playing with your hair or avoiding eye contact. This will only inflame an aggressive person. By maintaining an assertive stance you will also find that you will actually feel more assertive and therefore speak and act more appropriately (see also chapter 1).

Plan ahead

If you are going into a situation where you feel you need to be assertive, always plan ahead. Don't just turn up and say exactly what's on your mind; that could lead to many problems!

Consider the best time, think about your opening statement and potential replies (using the right words), think about how you will stand, your tone of voice. Have phrases ready as "get out clauses".

I appreciate that all this can seem very time consuming but it will really be worth it if the situation ends well. Also, when you do this regularly, it becomes easier and you would eventually do it almost automatically.

As a senior PA, you will no longer go into any tricky situations without a plan.

Notes:

Chapter 4:

Develop excellence and relationships through NLP

"Whether you think you can or whether you think you can't, you're right." Henry Ford

Chapter 4

Develop excellence and relationships through NLP

In this chapter we look at:

- What is NLP?
- Building rapport at four levels
- Non-verbal
- Voice and tonality
- Language
- Beliefs

NLP (neuro-linguistic programming) looks at how we think, communicate and behave. It is the study of human excellence and human experience.

The techniques are vital for a senior PA to carry out his/her role effectively. It enables the creation of rapport, enhances influencing skills, gives an understanding of how to create excellence and fully understand other people.

One of the most important aspects of NLP and of the PA role is the ability to build rapport with others. Rapport means "a close and harmonious relationship in which the people or groups concerned understand each other's feelings or ideas and communicate well".

As we have said, the role of the PA is now much more about building relationships than just tasks. Creating harmonious, valuable and effective relationships with colleagues, clients and others is an invaluable skill.

Some people can build rapport naturally; they are incredibly emotionally intelligent people. However, most need a bit of help.

We all naturally build rapport but, without understanding how it works, this rapport can just as easily be broken.

We build rapport at four levels:

1. Non-verbal: The instant we meet someone we start building rapport based on our body language (remember that is the 53% of how we read other's "messages"). If someone has similar body language to us, we feel a natural affinity towards them – rapport.

2. Voice/tonality: Of course, this is the 40% and so next in line. We feel comfortable with people whose tone of voice is similar to our own.

3. Language: This could be literally that we speak the same language as another person; immediately there is a rapport. However, it can also be that we use the same words due to a similar regional, educational or cultural background.

In the north of England, we call our evening meal tea, elsewhere it might be dinner or even supper.

Do you sit on a sofa, settee, couch or chaise-longue? Do you mow the lawn or cut the grass? All these say a great deal about a person. We can take this a step further; I'm going to come back to that later.

4. Beliefs: This is the final level to build rapport. We have similar body language and tone of voice as another person, we find we use similar words and now we find that we both play tennis! That's it – rapport.

Beliefs could, literally, be that you have the same religion as someone or perhaps the same ethics, high standards, political interests, family values, etc. It can also be that you both play the same sport, support the same team, read similar books and so on.

If we've reached all four levels, chances are it will be a successful relationship.

So this happens naturally and, where it doesn't, there can be conflict or, at least, lack of team work. What an emotionally intelligent PA will do is create that rapport by taking an interest in what interests the other person.

"Sit up and take notice of what makes the other person sit up and take notice!"

I am not for a moment suggesting hypocrisy or manipulation, I'm proposing that small changes in our behaviour can enhance relationships – and that has to be good.

Ashby's Law of Requisite Variety states,

"If you have more flexibility in your thoughts and behaviours than other people, then you can influence the outcome of the interactions with those people."

Case study

I once worked with a lady who was fairly quietly spoken, a very gentle person and very effective. However, I was young and still quite "bouncy" in my approach to people. Although I had never heard of Ashby or his law at that time, I realised I was a bit too much for her. Consequently I started to approach her more slowly and speak slightly more quietly. The result was our relationship blossomed.

A lot of conflict between managers and OPs comes from an aggressive manager "frightening" a less assertive assistant who then becomes very passive. This, in turn, irritates the manager and conflict arises. If the PA can slightly adapt his/her behaviour to be more assertive, to almost mirror the manager's body language and voice (without becoming aggressive), the relationship will improve.

Some people ask me though, "Why should I change? Why can't the other person change?" This is a good point but, given that someone has to change, why not be the "big one"?

Another presupposition of NLP is "If you always do what you've always done, you'll always get what you always got".

These techniques are taught to salespeople (hence the reason some people say it is manipulative). If you have rapport with someone you are more likely to buy from them.

However, I believe that if you are trying to improve a relationship, do a more effective job for your manager and resolve conflict, why is that a problem? We're not trying to make somebody do something they don't want to do; we're trying to improve the working environment.

**** Exercise ****

Think of a situation where you feel there is a poor rapport with somebody you work with. It may not be conflict but the relationship could be improved.

....

....

....

****

Let us now go back to language and we can take this a step further.

We all process information in different ways through our senses; we have our own preferences though – our dominant representational system.

Some people, artists, for example, may have a well-developed visual system or a musician an auditory preference.
Many people process information through their feelings (kinaesthetic). These VAK systems can be reflected in the words we use.

A visual person may use phrases such as "I see what you mean", an auditory person "That sounds good" and a kinaesthetic person "how do you feel about that?". If two people use similar VAK words, there will be a rapport. However, if you can spot the types of words a person uses, and use them as well, you can create rapport where it may not have existed.

This advanced technique can ultimately lead to a resolution or even avoidance of conflict, more effective relationships and hence an improved working environment. This does not happen easily but have a go.

Of course, in writing it is much easier to spot the different types of words and you can then use similar words, even just using the same sign off as the person to whom you are replying.

Here are some example words people might use:

Visual	Auditory	Kinaesthetic
look	audible	feel
appear	sounds like	handle
seem	remark	emotional
clarity	listen	sensitive
envision	speechless	affected
illustrate	ring	active
scene	noise	pressure
clear	ear shot	shallow
perspective	mention	hunch
reveal	loud	heated
focus	hear	smooth
view	like a bell	throw out
bright	tune in	handle on
picture	singing	in touch

**** Exercise ****

Write a note to three different people (one visual, one auditory and one kinaesthetic) to ask them to give you an idea of this month's sales figures:

(There are suggestions at the back of the book.)

....

....

....

....

....

....

****

"The meaning of your communication is the response you get back, regardless of the intention."

If someone has not understood us, we often become frustrated and consider the person unhelpful or even stupid. However, NLP teaches us that we should look at this differently; perhaps the person didn't understand because we didn't explain it from their perspective.

An emotionally intelligent PA will never assume that someone hasn't understood because they are stupid. They will consider the way they phrased their communication and rephrase it in a more appropriate way – taking the listener into consideration.

"If what you are doing isn't working, do something else."

**** Exercise ****

You ask a junior member of staff to do some filing. After a couple of days it still hasn't been done. The automatic reaction is to assume the person is lazy, doesn't care, is being unhelpful, etc. What other reasons might an emotionally intelligent PA consider?

(See the end of the book for some ideas.)

....

....

....

....

....

....

****

"The map is not the territory."

This is another favourite presupposition of mine. If you imagine a simple map of Nepal and you want to estimate the time to travel between two cities. You look at the distance and think it may only take a few hours; however, there are no contour lines and, in fact, Mount Everest is between these two cities...

How can we know what something is really like if we haven't been there, or experienced it?

A successful PA will have probably worked his/her way up the organisation, or through various organisations. As well as various products and/or services, they will also have experienced different management styles, corporate cultures and working practices.

Case study

An extremely successful company CEO I know from many years ago when he was a graduate trainee, had complained about having to work "on the shop floor". I am convinced that it was that basic knowledge of the business that enabled him to become a highly respected and efficacious corporate tycoon. He knew "the territory". Successful management comes from either experience at "shop floor" level or from collaboration with those who are in "the territory".

An effective PA, who remember has the same objectives as the manager, will be aware of this and will familiarise him/herself with everybody's working situation. They will also encourage their manager to stop looking at "the map" and get into "the territory".

Furthermore, the realisation that things may not be how you interpret them shows incredible emotional intelligence and you can become the fabulous PA you want to be.

How does your manager learn about the "territory"?
Do you think he/she could do more?
If so, what could you suggest?

....

....

....

....

....

....

****

"There is no failure only feedback."

NLP teaches us that, just because something hasn't worked, it doesn't mean we have failed; it means we have found a way that doesn't work and have probably learnt from the experience as well.

There are many inspiring Thomas Edison quotes and here is one that sums up the no failure idea:

"I have not failed. I've just found 10,000 ways that won't work".

He also said,

*"Negative results are just what I want.
They're just as valuable to me as positive results. I can never find the thing that does the job best until I find the ones that don't."*

If something doesn't work out, never consider yourself a failure; try something different and learn from the mistake. Under different circumstances, that could be the right answer.

Do you feel you have failed at anything? If so, how could you turn this into a lesson learnt or even a positive? How can you now move on and not feel disillusioned?

....

....

....

....

....

....

****

Remember that you have the choice of how to react. By choosing to let things upset us, get angry, give up, etc, we are only hurting ourselves and letting others win. We are causing ourselves pain, stress and consequently, wasting time, energy and ruining our image.

Choose to react professionally; stay calm, reframe negatives into positives, if you can't change the situation, go with the flow. I remember a guy on a plane I was taking which was delayed leaving because of ice on the wings. He became so angry with the aircrew (probably he was very nervous about flying) and said he would be late for his meeting. My thought was that being late for the meeting was probably the better option than trying to take off with frozen wings....

And finally on this topic:

> *"We have an old saying in Delta House: don't get mad, get even."* Animal House

Notes:

Chapter 5:

Manage staff successfully

"Success in management requires learning
as fast as the world is changing."
Warren Bennis

Chapter 5
Manage staff successfully

In this chapter we look at:

* Recruitment

* Delegation

* Avoid bullying behaviour

* How to motivate your staff

Many OPs are involved in the recruitment of other OPs, administrators and even their own assistants.

Hiring can be a minefield and it is usually a good idea to use a reputable recruitment company to help you. Beware of companies who just send any old candidate as they think this looks as though they are doing a good job.

A top-class recruitment company will filter candidates based on your requirements. That means you must ensure you prepare a detailed job description and person specification. When preparing this, it is vital to think not just about the business now but also where you anticipated the business going.

Another common means of finding staff is recommendation, although, always remember the person who suits one manager or company, may not suit another.

Advertising is another means, but this can be expensive. Today, organisations are turning more and more to social media (including looking at candidates' personal Facebook accounts...).

If you would like to know more about recruitment, I can recommend "The Book on Recruitment" by Carole Fossey.

So, you have found your ideal candidate, they've accepted the job and they are now working with you.

From day one you should ensure everyone is clear about the person's role, responsibilities and authority. This, of course, should have been discussed at the interview stage and it should now be formalised on arrival in the company.

Make sure all the new person's colleagues also understand the role. This could be a good time to verify that everyone in the organisation has clear and specific objectives, tasks and authority.

Introduce the new person to his/her main colleagues and let them start to get to know each other and become creative.

Ensure they are fully au fait with company culture, dress, customs, etc. Inform them of the main objectives for their role for the first week. At the end of the week, take the time to discuss those objectives, achievements, difficulties, challenges and the next steps.

**** Exercise ****

In your organisation specifically, what would a new person need to learn?

....
....
....
....
....
....

****

When you are delegating to somebody always make sure they are fully briefed, that they understand the objectives of their tasks. Encourage questions and then don't stand over them.

If someone reports to you, they should be fully conversant with your objectives; they are his/her objectives too.

**** Exercise ****

What are your objectives?

What are your manager's objectives?

....
....
....
....
....
....

****

Delegation

Delegate authority rather than individual tasks, for example, rather than continually asking a junior administrator to do photocopies, give him/her responsibility for all copying. This will also enable them to learn to manage their workload.

Delegation is an important part of training.

Don't apologise for delegating, unless it is a particularly onerous task. Be assertive and trust the person to do their job.

Give feedback in a positive manner. Rather than saying "you made a mess of that letter, it's full of spelling mistakes", say "thank you for doing the letter; there are some spelling mistakes so we need to talk about the standard of letters that we issue, but it's well laid out."

Even if the feedback is good, it is motivating for a person to understand why they did a good job and could this lead to more responsibility or development of their role.

You may want to build in safeguards (giving a slightly earlier deadline for example) while you are building trust.

Remember that possessive feelings about work are negative and unproductive. Keeping hold of minor tasks impedes the development of effective management.

The main reason people are unwilling to delegate is because it involves the loss of direct control, but the retention of overall responsibility.

If you ever have disciplinary or other issues with a member of staff who reports to you, always make sure you discuss the problems with them in the first instance in private. You may need a witness at a later, more formal stage. Never let anyone feel humiliated; it won't help to solve the initial problem.

Get their input on why there are problems; it may be that you don't fully appreciate their situation.

When the problem is established, collaborate on finding a viable solution.

Jenny, who is very good at her job usually, has been showing some reluctance to attend meetings on behalf of her manager. Frances, the manager, is rather disappointed in her attitude.

When she speaks to Jenny, she learns that a previous unpleasant experience in a meeting, when someone ridiculed her suggestion, made her nervous about going again.

How could this be resolved?

....

....

....

....

....

....

****

Avoid bullying behaviour

Some people can be "difficult". Before going in with criticism or even anger, ask yourself why they may be like that. Remember emotional intelligence; we don't know the other person's story. Communication is vital to mutual understanding and happy working relationships.

If, however, the member of staff is not responding, further action may need to be taken and it is important to discuss with HR experts to ensure the correct procedures are followed (http://www.bakerthompsonassoc.co.uk/news-resources/campaigns).

Avoid bullying at all costs. Happy workers are effective workers. (Read more on being bullied later.)

How do we know if we are bullying and what can we do to ensure our staff are happy and effective?

"I don't bully my staff, but, if I don't shout at them they won't do the job."

Maybe they don't do the job because they have no respect for the manager, because the manager hasn't explained the objectives clearly or because they are frightened of making a mistake and being shouted at more.

A true leader (which is what a manager should be) will instil motivation into his/her staff. Leaders ensure their team is fully briefed, is aware of the objectives and deadlines. They use praise for success to motivate, rather than criticism for mistakes to demotivate. Any necessary criticism is delivered in as positive a manner as possible.

You know your staff feel bullied if:

- they aren't proactive
- they don't make eye contact with you
- they have very passive body language
- they have trouble expressing themselves to you
- they stop talking when you walk in the room
- there is a bad atmosphere in the office
- nobody is willing to put in extra hours
- productivity is low
- absences are common
- staff turnover is high
- vacancies are always filled from outside the organisation
- there's no laughter in the workplace

How to motivate your staff:

✓ ensure their health and safety
✓ include them in projects
✓ ensure collaboration; ask for their views
✓ praise their successes
✓ show total respect for the person
✓ don't immediately criticise their ideas; encourage creativity
✓ give negative feedback privately (see more below)
✓ ensure a pleasant working environment (good desks, plants, light, etc.)
✓ ensure your body language and tone of voice, as well as your words, aren't aggressive
✓ encourage team working; don't create divisions
✓ encourage laughter

Of course, people make mistakes and sometimes more than are acceptable. However, negative feedback should always be given privately and constructively. Tell the person what they are doing wrong and the impact that this is having or may have.

Ask them why they think they made the mistake and how they feel they could rectify it; people will be much more willing to improve if it's their idea.

Watch out for the words "just" and "but" as in "I'm just saying" or "You did a great job but...". Replace the "but" with an "and". "You did a great job and when we sort the parking problem it will be terrific" - so much more motivating.

Use the word "yet"; as in "you've not got it right .... yet".

Finally, I mentioned laughter because I feel it is a vital part of an effective working environment. It relieves stress, builds teams and means your clients are interacting with happy people; what is there to lose?

Some companies have a culture of bullying; it starts from the top. It is based on the belief that people are more effective under pressure. Many people do perform better under pressure but it should be positive pressure, not negative.

Ensure staff have regular evaluations, but don't wait for those to resolve any issues. Evaluations should never hold surprises. Evaluations are also not just about the past performance, they are a tool for planning future responsibilities and roles.

OPs can be in many different roles; working as a PA to a director, for example, and also being an Office Manager. They may manage their own secretary/administrator who assists with the day to day running of the office, whilst the PA works more closely with the Executive, perhaps including attending meetings on his/her behalf.

Notes:

Chapter 6:
Be a great leader

"The quality of a leader is reflected in the standards they set for themselves."

Ray Kroc

Chapter 6:
Be a great leader

In this chapter we look at:

- What is leadership?
- The difference between managing and leading
- Motivation
- Making decisions under pressure
- Avoiding and resolving conflict

What is leadership?

It's the process of influencing the behaviour or attitudes of others, of getting the best out of people, individually and collectively.

I love this quotation attributed to Dwight Eisenhower (former President of the USA):

"Leadership is the art of getting someone else to do something you want done because he wants to do it."

What is the difference between managing and leading?

A manager may not necessarily be a leader (sadly) and a leader may not necessarily be a manager; it could just as easily be a PA.

Anyone can be a leader by showing the right attributes and qualities and by achieving the objectives above.

What are these qualities?

A leader will have most of, if not all, these attributes:

- ✓ Business acumen
- ✓ Knows how to build rapport
- ✓ Excellent communication skills
- ✓ Good listener
- ✓ Empathetic
- ✓ Team player
- ✓ Understands people
- ✓ Decision maker
- ✓ Emotionally intelligent
- ✓ Self-belief
- ✓ Visibility
- ✓ Integrity
- ✓ Commitment
- ✓ Vision
- ✓ Ability to inspire and motivate

The first three we have looked at already, others will be raised at various points in the book.

Motivation

To inspire people to work effectively and produce excellent results, it is vital to find out what motivates them. It was once assumed that motivation came from outside; we now know that we can also motivate ourselves

Years ago many employers thought that you had to be strict with staff to make them work well; you had to punish mistakes, "command and control". Of course, today, most organisations are aware of the power of "advise and consent". Rewarding good work is much more effective than punishing bad work.

Unfortunately, I meet many PAs and administrators whose managers still take the "stick" route rather than the "carrot". This creates an unhappy environment, demotivated staff, dysfunctional organisations and consequently, failing businesses.

The bullies become stressed, unhappy and tired and they could so easily make life better for everyone – and more effective and successful.

Maslow's Hierarchy of Needs explains people's motivation:

morality, creativity, spontaneity, problem solving, lack of prejudice, acceptance of facts	5	Self-actualization
self-esteem, confidence, achievement, respect of others, respect by others	4	Self-esteem
friendship, family, sexual intimacy, sense of connection	3	Love and belonging
security of body, employment, resources, morality, family, health, property	2	Safety and security
breathing, food, sex, sleep, homeostasis, excretion	1	Physiological needs

If we have the basics in place (food, drink, air and sleep), we are then able to move to the next level and so on. It is therefore only possible to be the best we can be if all the other stages are in place.

It is difficult for a person to be motivated in their work if, for example, they have financial or relationship worries at home or if they have taken a blow to their confidence at some point.

More recent research suggests that Family/Friendships should, in fact, be lower in the pyramid as those relationships are vital to our well-being. We very much need other people.

As an emotionally intelligent leader, a PA would recognise this and always consider the reasons why another person may act in a certain way. Just because we feel very comfortable doing something, that doesn't mean another person will feel the same. Remember, we don't always know their story.

Motivators vary from person to person. There is money which enables all the basics in the pyramid. We are also motivated by colleagues, the work environment, the content of the role, and successes. You may have specific aspects of your role that really drive you ahead.

**** Exercise ****

What particularly motivates you?

....

....

....

What do you think motivates your manager and colleagues?

....

....

....

****

At the top of the pyramid it's confidence and respect that motivate us. If we have those we can excel.

Remember, though, this book is not just about you; it's also about your manager and your colleagues. An emotionally intelligent PA will understand what motivates her manager and her co-workers. By understanding that, a top PA can become an influential leader.

We will be looking at more of the leadership qualities later in the book.

> *"You shouldn't blindly accept a leader's advice. You've got to question leaders on occasion." Richard Branson*

Making decisions under pressure

OPs are making decisions continually during a normal working day. These can be big or small, but most have to be taken under pressure.

In some circumstances a PA may have time to reflect and make well-informed decisions. What is the process for doing this?

✓ Identify issues;

✓ Undertake analysis;

✓ Evaluate options;

✓ Identify choices;

✓ Implement plans.

Decisions will be based on knowledge, past experience or perhaps costs.

However, often a proactive PA will consult colleagues, managers or other appropriate contacts to ensure they are fully informed to make the choice.

Of course, it is possible to ask the manager, but so often they are away or in meetings. Also, a proactive PA will want to provide their manager with viable solutions rather than problems.

There are two good bases to use if you need to make a decision under pressure:

1. What are your manager's objectives and which option fits best with those?

2. Which option would give the best outcome for the success of the organisation?

OPs should always know their manager's objectives; they are the PA's objectives too. You and your manager do the same job, you simply do different tasks to achieve those objectives.

However, in a typical hectic environment where a PA may work, there is often little time to go through the reflection and consultation process. Of course, the two questions above will help with the split second decision but there is another technique.

An effective PA will usually have a Plan B. When planning for speakers, trips, conferences, document circulation, for example, the possibility of something going awry should always be considered and a potential solution identified.

**** Exercise ****

Think of a situation where you may need a plan B.

What is your plan?

....

....

....

....

****

Avoiding and resolving conflict

The workplace is full of people with differing views, attitudes and beliefs; consequently, there will be conflict. A truly emotionally intelligent PA will understand this and will also know how to avoid and/or deal with it.

We have already looked at assertiveness, NLP techniques, managing staff and being a leader. We are going to look at emotional intelligence in more depth later. All these skills enable an excellent PA to manage any conflict that may arise.

Do you want the window open or closed, music on or off? You talk too much, too loudly. Heating on or off? These are all apparently small issues that may become extremely contentious.

Of course, it can also be differences of opinion on working practice, business decisions, management and so on. Most difficult of all, it can be personality clashes and relationship problems that cause the conflict.

It can simply be someone "got out of bed the wrong side"!

The conflict can be with colleagues or with your manager; both are important to resolve.

The most important way to avoid conflict is by regular, honest communication. Immediately a problem arises, the parties should speak about the issues and listen to each other and empathise to find a potential compromise, if not a solution.

The longer the conflict goes on without being discussed, the worse the situation will become.

If necessary, get a third party to mediate. Get another perspective.

Understand that the other person's story is very different from yours. Make every effort to understand why they think as they do.

Build rapport by finding a common belief. You could start by agreeing that you both want the success of the organisation, that conflict will not help that and you should both do everything possible to help achieve it. Find the common ground to work together on.

Accept the conflict, don't deny it and move on to find solutions.

Listen to each other and put yourself in their place; accept that we are not always right just because we believe something. That's exactly what the other person thinks...

If you are more senior than the other person, or you have to do something on behalf of your manager, make sure that the person understands why something has to be done.

It is often a challenge, particularly in some cultures, that people don't appreciate the role of the assistant. People say "why are you asking for this why isn't your manager asking me?" They don't realise that an assistant asks on behalf on their manager ... seems obvious, I know, but it is all part of the education needed on the role of the PA.

If appropriate, ask for the other person's opinion on alternatives; remember you don't always know everything.

"What could we do to resolve this?" This is a much better way to approach a situation than "This is what you are going to do."

Sadly, over the years I have been training, I hear of many instances of PAs and administrators being bullied, usually by their managers. Unfortunately, I also experienced this myself as a young PA.

Abuse may not be physical (and often isn't). It can be verbal - psychological. It may even be that the bullied person is ignored; recent studies showed that exclusion is considered the worst type of bullying.

Often the bully is a manager which makes it difficult for the person to stand up for their rights.

I have seen, and, sadly, experienced such behaviour. It is demoralising, depressing and can impact on performance, self-esteem and health.

Bullies are aggressive; this may be because they feel insecure themselves or perhaps they are just not nice people. If you act in an aggressive manner towards them the situation could become nasty and spiral out of control. It would also mean you are no better than your bully.

On the other hand, if you are too passive this irritates the bully and makes them even more aggressive. The problem is that most administrators become passive because of their fear of the bully - often their manager or someone in a more senior position.

Case study

David hired Jane as his PA. After the first week he was so delighted with her that he held a small party on the Friday evening to celebrate her arrival. Everything seemed to be going very well.

However, gradually he changed. Jane had always been confident in her roles, but this was a new industry, a much more stressful environment and a totally different culture from those she had been used to. She found it hard to acclimatise and probably appeared nervous, although she worked hard to fit in and "learn the ropes".

Instead of giving support and helping her to learn ("too busy"), David turned against her and told her to speak to other people about how to do things. He then started ignoring her, unless it was to criticise. She heard him complaining about her in the corridor and, finally, the ultimate humiliation, he got her out of the office on a pretext so he could speak to another PA about working for him. Jane was moved on.

Although young and less experienced at the time, eventually all turned out extremely well for Jane through the support of more reasonable people ... it could have been very different. She now campaigns against bullying.

It is essential to deal with bullies in an assertive manner. Speak to your tormentor in a calm, polite and civilised way. Explain that you feel unhappy when they speak to you in a certain way or behave towards you in a particular manner. Do not accuse them of bullying you, just tell them how they make you feel.

If possible, share your experiences with a colleague or a Human Resources member of staff. It may then be necessary to follow the organisation's grievance procedures.

Act as quickly as possible against the bully; it becomes more difficult as they drain you of confidence. Remember, a person can only make you feel inferior with your permission ......

If the bullying continues, it is important to keep a diary of events and then to contact some of the experts whose websites are listed below:

www.workplacebullying.co.uk

http://www.workplacebullying.org/

www.jfo.org.uk

There are also quite a few Twitter accounts about bullying. Why not follow these:

@bulliedbyboss

@bullyinguk

@StopBullyingNow

Chapter 7:
Network successfully

"Effective networking isn't a result of luck
- it requires hard work and persistence."
Lewis Howes

Chapter 7:
Network successfully

In this chapter we look at:

*   Reasons to network
*   Plan your strategy
*   Follow up

We have already said that the PA role nowadays is much more relationship focused than task focused.

A modern day PA will become involved in networking for various reasons:

✓ to help their manager
✓ to help themselves
✓ to help others
✓ to learn
✓ to share
✓ to develop

Firstly by meeting other OPs, managers, clients, etc, the PA is establishing connections which may, in future, enable him/her to do a better job for the manager - making connections who can help your manager gain access to information, events, and potential new business. These contacts may also be helpful if you decided to change jobs.

The PA is able to "use" the connections to gain information, access, etc.

The PA will learn from other OPs and experts in particular

fields; this enables them to become a better PA and also enhances their personal and professional development.

It is important to remember, too, that it is not just about "what's in it for me?". OPs who are true leaders will want to help other people just as much. Whilst being aware of confidentiality, it is great to share skills, techniques and tips with others. You could also introduce people to help them get jobs or gain business.

We meet people all the time, and most of us enjoy that. However, as soon as the word "networking" comes up, people decide they don't like it at all. This is often because it feels forced and because it's in a business situation.

If you go to networking events with a view that you are going to meet people who you may be able to help and to learn new things, you will feel much more relaxed and will never be disappointed.

As with everything the PA does, you should prepare for the event. Find out who will be there and see if there are people you would particularly like to meet – perhaps you have spoken to them on the 'phone, but never met them, for example.

Plan your strategy; how will you introduce yourself? Will you approach groups or people on their own or in pairs? Have some topics of conversation ready. Some questions you may ask are:

- What is your connection to the organiser?
- Where have you come from today?
- Tell me about your business
- Have you been to this venue before?
- What do you think of the venue?
- What is your interest in the topic of the speaker today?

Notice they are open questions and, therefore, instigate more discussion and you will learn more.

Part of your preparation might be to find out about people you don't know so you can ask appropriate questions, or remember things that people you have met have told you previously. You can then ask how the holiday went, are their children enjoying the new school, etc.

When you are asked questions, answer briefly and turn the conversation back to the other person to learn more.

People really appreciate it when you care about and take an interest in them.

Listen carefully too; take an interest. Don't allow yourself to be distracted by other people. Find ways you could help others.

Often people are nervous when they arrive at events. It is good to look around the room before you actually go in. See if there is anyone you know or anyone who is alone. A person who is alone will very likely be delighted that you have initiated the conversation.

If those aren't options then look for pairs or groups that have open body language (not huddled in deep discussion). Walk up, smiling, and ask "do you mind if I join you?". It is unlikely you will not be made welcome. They may immediately do introductions or you may have to wait a few moments as someone finishes a story, for example.

When you are introducing yourself, say your first name and then repeat it with your surname. I would say, "Hello, I'm Heather, Heather Baker". This reinforces your name and helps the other person remember. Wear your name badge on the right so it's clearly visible as your turn to shake hands. And make sure your handshake is firm, without crushing anyone. A limp handshake is a definite "no no".

Have a short phrase ready to explain what your role is and, perhaps, why you are attending the event.

In all the above situations, do NOT apologise!

Make sure you have plenty of business cards printed to take along; you want to be able to give others your details in an easy and professional manner. Collect business cards from other people so you can keep in touch and add them to your network of social media contacts too. Ideally, ask someone for their card first and don't start dishing out your cards immediately you arrive. If you travel for business, ensure you are aware of business card etiquette as well as all other cultural differences. In Singapore, for example, the handing over of a business card is done in a very formal manner, presenting it to the other person with both hands. The recipient should then take some time to read the card and comment. There are now apps for collecting people's details and this is another available option.

**** Exercise ****

Practise at home how you would walk up to people and introduce yourself.

Prepare some relevant questions to start a conversation.

....

....

....

....

****

Look professional in your dress and appearance; make sure you wear comfortable shoes – you may have to stand for a while.

I can recommend "Eat, Drink & Succeed" by Laura Schwartz to learn much more.

Remember that you have networking opportunities not just at specific networking events, but also at training courses, conferences and parties. An emotionally intelligent PA will also want to network within the organisation and at all levels.

Nowadays social media is also a major part of networking. Facebook, LinkedIn, Twitter, etc are all ways of "meeting" and collaborating with others. Even though it is online, all the same professional standards should apply.

Ideally, join online social networking groups such as the Executive Secretary Magazine group on LinkedIn which has thousands of members – office professionals from around the world.

Finally, whenever you had met or LinkedIn with someone, always follow up with messages and keep the contact going.

Chapter 8:

Ensure positive perceptions

A strong, positive self-image is the best possible preparation for success.
Joyce Brothers

Chapter 8:
Ensure positive perceptions

In this chapter we look at:

- Perceptions of PAs
- Modelling behaviour

Sadly, over the years, perceptions of PAs and administrators have been very negative. Things are improving but not as quickly as we would like.

The history of these perceptions comes from the fact that, in the early and mid-20th century, the majority of people in these roles were women, who were often looked down on in the workplace.

I see many occasions of senior consultants, professors, company directors etc. who, because the administrators do not always have as high academic qualifications (e.g., a degree), consider their assistants as less valuable. In fact PAs and administrators are usually much more capable and qualified with organisational and interpersonal skills – all just as valuable, but different.

It is an old-fashioned idea that administration is of less importance. Happily, many organisations and their managers and directors now recognise and understand the value of these employees.

Those who still harbour negative perceptions not only cause offence to the administrators and demean them, they also disadvantage their own position because a PA can do so much to help their manager succeed; that is their role.

However, one of the biggest stumbling blocks is the fact that many PAs and administrators reinforce these negative perceptions with their behaviour and the way they react to the negativity.

If we are treated like children, we tend to behave like children. This can be overcome by changing our reactions.

In any situation we all have a choice of how we react. Some people choose to react negatively, passively or aggressively; some choose positivity and assertiveness. It is not easy, however, to choose the positive option when people are treating us with negativity.

Let's start with some basic problems. How many times have you heard people say "oh, she's just a secretary"? Unhappily, I have also heard people say "oh, I'm just a secretary". That word "just" being used again to demean someone or ourselves. Remember we talked about the words we use and the impression that these can give. Never include the word "just" when you give your job title or describe what you do.

PAs and administrators should use positive language to ensure positive perceptions.

**** Exercise ****

Think of positive ways to explain what you do.

....

....

****

Don't put yourself down; if you can't do something, keep quiet and get trained. Accept compliments gracefully; if someone tells you that you look smart or have done a good job, then say thank you. It's also advisable to model people's behaviour. If there are people in your organisation that you admire or aspire to be like, watch and listen to how they behave and speak. Chat with them to get the benefit of their wisdom and experience. There's no need to change who you are, just add their skills and qualities to your repertoire.

**** Exercise ****

Who could I look to as a model? Why?

....

....

****

I used to answer the 'phone, for example, "good morning, Mr Bennett's office; Heather speaking", until a female senior manager pointed out that I should use my surname (have you noticed how junior administrators "never have surnames"?). I tried it; "good morning, Mr Bennett's office; Heather Baker speaking".

I felt more confident; people changed how they interacted with me and I also found that people would ask me questions other than "is he there?".

Let's look again at how our reaction to other people's behaviour can help reinforce positive perceptions. A PA in an insurance company once told me that she was upset by her manager's attitude when she returned from attending a PA quarterly lunch meeting. He always said "Have you had a nice little jolly then?" This was incredibly patronising. As she said, he goes on lunches nearly every day and those are considered business lunches, her quarterly meeting was considered a "little jolly". "What could I do?" she asked me.

I asked her how she responded when he said this and she admitted she would just laugh... going along with his "joke". I proposed that, if he said it again, she say "yes, thank you; it was very interesting and I have some ideas to put to you" (or something similar). It's called "speaking like an adult".

Think of an occasion when you would like to
respond more positively and how you would do this

. . . .

. . . .

. . . .

. . . .

******

Case study

Martyn, who was a successful PA for many years, said
this when I asked how it felt being in a role which is very
female dominated:

"My first PA role was working for a female Professor who
had worked in the University for most of her life and had
worked with a number of PAs - all of whom were women.
I found this an interesting stage for both of us because it
was a clean slate and I could make the role my own and
she found it really refreshing to work with a male PA for
a change. Although the whole environment was female
dominated I was a welcome addition to that and often
found myself in place to diffuse mood swings which I was
told had been a problem with other PAs in the past!"

"My second PA role was for three Professors, again all of
them had previously had female PAs so I was able to bring
a fresh approach to their working cultures. I frequently
surprised people when they learnt that the Profs had a
male PA - more often than not it was a pleasant surprise for
them."

Martyn feels that an advantage of being a male PA is that it
made people question some of the dated expectations and
improved many people's behaviour towards PAs.

Have you heard of visualisation? It is the means whereby we see in our minds what we want to achieve. For example, if we are doing a presentation, visualisation can help us prepare. See yourself speaking in front of the group, see yourself getting lots of attention and praise and you will feel more confident on the day.

Many sports people use visualisation; they run a race in their mind over and over again. They see themselves winning and this improves their chances of success.

Before you go into tricky meetings or interviews, visualise it going well.

So, where do you want to be? How does that person dress, how do they walk, how do they speak, how do they behave? Then become that person. Don't listen to those fearful voices that tell you that you can't do something.

Remember that you are as important as all colleagues. Even if you are not at a high level in the organisation, your skills are still vital to help everyone succeed. Don't put yourself down and don't let people make you feel inferior – they can only do that if you let them.

Finally, remember body language... the most important aspect. Walk, stand and sit as a professional, confident and assertive PA.

Chapter 9: Develop your emotional intelligence

"Emotional intelligence is your ability to recognise and understand emotions in yourself and others, and your ability to use this awareness to manage your behaviour and relationships." Travis Bradberry

Chapter 9: Develop your emotional intelligence

In this chapter we look at:

- Emotional intelligence
- Other people
- Communicate your needs
- Feedback
- Influence
- Avoiding conflict
- Team work
- Flexibility

Emotional intelligence is essential for any PA to be successful. Building relationships is a large part of a senior PA/EA's role... but what does it entail?

An emotional intelligent PA:

- ✓ understands other people
- ✓ can express themselves with clarity
- ✓ can assert their needs
- ✓ exchanges constructive feedback
- ✓ is able to influence other people
- ✓ can avoid and resolve conflict
- ✓ is a great team member, and
- ✓ is flexible

Let's take each one individually:

Understands other people

Let's reflect on communications, covered earlier.

An emotionally intelligent PA doesn't just listen to the words people are saying, they listen to the tone of voice as well and, of course, watch the body language. As we showed in chapter 1, body language and tone of voice give us the most information about what a person is truly thinking and/or feeling.

So an emotionally intelligent PA will listen and observe. They do not jump to conclusions nor make subjective decisions and assumptions based on their feelings and experiences. They "walk in the other person's shoes". The map is not the territory.

They remember that not everyone has the same story; we don't all come to situations with the same history.

We inwardly question why somebody says or does something; not automatically assuming they're wrong and we're right.

An emotionally intelligent PA will also not assume something is always their fault. It is easy to be defensive, particularly with a bullying manager, and assume that the manager is cross at us. It may just be that we are the nearest person when they are angry and we often then receive the backlash – not fair, of course, but it happens.

Thinking carefully about other people's actions and statements can ensure relationships are not damaged and are, in fact, improved.

**** Exercise ****

Think of an occasion when you have assumed another person was in the wrong; could they have been right? How else could you have interpreted their behaviour?

....

....

....

****

Just because you're right, it doesn't mean the other person is wrong.

Can express themselves with clarity

Remember we established earlier that "the meaning of my communication is the response I get back, regardless of my intention?" That is what this section reinforces.

A truly emotionally intelligent PA will always consider the other person before speaking; weighing up what would be the best way to express themselves to make the other person feel valued and not undermined in any way.

They will "speak the other person's language"; both literally and figuratively. This means using words they will understand, citing references that will mean something to them. You will consider if they may be visual, auditory or kinaesthetic. Like "the genius of David Beckham", you will "pass to the other player in the way that player likes to receive the ball".

If the other person hasn't understood, the emotionally intelligent PA doesn't just repeat him/herself louder, they find other words.

**** Exercise ****

Next time you have to explain something to somebody, think about how you can make your explanation appropriate to that person.

....

....

....

....

****

Can assert their needs

The emotionally intelligent PA is assertive (see chapter 3)

Exchanges constructive feedback

Nowadays, many PAs and EAs have assistants themselves or manage teams of administrators. It is vital, if you wish to be seen as an effective leader, to give feedback in a constructive manner; considering how to express themselves with clarity.

Even those who don't manage staff may have to give feedback to managers, colleagues or clients. Again, it is vital not to get this wrong.

You will remember from our chapter on assertiveness, we discussed how to speak to the work experience person in your office who has typed a letter full of spelling mistakes. This is a first example of how to give good feedback. We didn't make the young person feel worthless and gave encouragement.

The words we use are very important too. Remember we looked at avoiding the word "but".

When you give feedback make sure negative comments are given privately. It is very bad leadership to criticise someone in front of other people. Ask them for their opinion on why something went wrong and get them to propose ways to put things right.

Don't dwell on what has happened and can't be changed; instead focus on what can be done in the future.

**** Exercise ****

Think of the feedback you have to offer. Find a way to make it even better using some of the techniques above.

....

....

....

....

****

Is able to influence other people

Given the impact of emotionally intelligent behaviour, you will find yourself able to influence the outcome of interactions. Because you are prepared to change your behaviour in small ways, you will find people much more amenable to your needs.

Don't nag; ask them to remind you. Learn to understand their priorities.

**** Exercise ****

How could you influence someone to do something for you at work?

....

....

....

....

****

Can avoid and resolve conflict

Because of their emotional intelligence, a PA who is a leader will be less involved in conflict themselves, will be able to diffuse conflict between others and, if conflict does occur, will know how to remedy things.

Given the excellent communication skills, a PA will also consider how they express themselves and therefore don't cause offence. They will listen carefully to fully understand people and so will seem empathetic rather than aggressive to other people.

With excellent assertive skills, the PA will maintain control of their workload, while not upsetting other people.

Because they understand that "the map is not the territory" they will consider other people's point of view rather than making assumptions.

Is a great team member

With good communications, leadership and assertiveness skills a PA will be able to work effectively with other people.

Is flexible

Finally, the emotionally intelligent leader is prepared to change their behaviour to ensure excellent relationships. They won't say "well, why can't they make the first move?" or "why should I apologise?". They will find ways to end conflicts and work excellently with others.

Notes:

Chapter 10:
Set goals

"Discipline is the bridge between goals and accomplishment." Jim Rohn

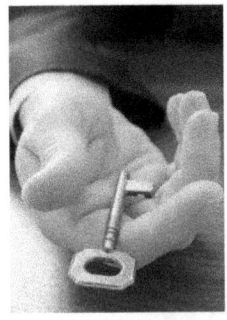

Chapter 10:
Set goals

In this chapter we look at:

- Beliefs
- Defining your goals
- CAN DO

We've all done it – dreamed of a top job, an exotic holiday or a catwalk figure – yet, how often do these things come to fruition?

"When we've got a bit of money, we'll go on a really nice holiday."

"I've always fancied working abroad."

"I'd love a job like that."

"I wish I were thinner."

And I'm sure you can think of many more! We've all done it – dreamed of a top job, an exotic holiday or a catwalk figure – yet, how often do these things come to fruition? We sit and wait for money to drop from the sky, for weight to miraculously disappear or the MD to walk into our office and offer us our dream job. It won't happen; we have to make things happen.

Quite a few people have told me how lucky I am to do the work I do – I appreciate their comments, but there wasn't really a great deal of luck involved. It was down to picking a course I enjoyed after school, working hard to get qualifications, applying for jobs I wanted, taking opportunities if they came up by chance and making opportunities if they didn't.

The only thing that's stopping you from achieving your ambition is probably you.

One of the main obstacles is our limiting beliefs; those are literally beliefs that limit us. Examples might be:

- ✗ I've never been any good at ...
- ✗ Nobody would take me seriously
- ✗ I'm not good enough
- ✗ I can never do ...
- ✗ I'm no good at ...
- ✗ Everybody else is so much better/important/confident than me
- ✗ Computers hate me

**** Exercise ****

Turn these beliefs into empowering beliefs.

....

....

....

....

****

OK, so, first step; how can you make that dream come true if you don't know what it is? Oh yes, we know vaguely (see the opening quotes), but that's not good enough. Let's take each of those desires and make them specific:

"When we've got a bit of money, we'll go on a really nice holiday."

"When we have £3,000 then we can holiday for two weeks in Barcelona."

"I've always fancied working abroad."

"I want to do my current job, but in Paris."

"I'd love a job like that."

"I want to work as a PA to a television executive."

"I wish I were thinner."

"I want to be a size 12 again."

So, now we're getting somewhere; now we know precisely what we want we can start to work out how to get it. Let's take Barcelona (seems like a good idea to me!). We now have a focus to work on. We need £3,000; how long will it take us to save that, or when do we want to go to Barcelona? Let's say we want to go in 12 months' time. You probably have to pay for the holiday a couple of months before leaving so let's say 10 months (it's easier maths that way too!). We have to save £300 a month. Is that feasible? If yes, go for it; if not, change the plan or go later. Once that's in place, you're almost on your way.

- How about your current job in Paris?
- Does your type of work exist in Paris?
- Do you speak French? If not, what can you do to learn, or should you look at another location where English is spoken?
- Where are jobs advertised?
- Have your joined relevant groups on LinkedIn?
- Are you a member of a world-wide networking organisation such as IMA (www.ima-network.org)?
- Where would you live – could you afford it?

- Does your organisation have branches overseas?

Some of the questions below may also apply? Don't forget to anticipate challenges – what may be the barriers to achieving your goal? How would you cope with these? What would enable you to battle through?

Let's look now at the PA to a TV executive (or this could be any job you want). Ask yourself some questions:

- What qualifications are necessary, and do I have them?
- If I don't have them, how can I get them?
- Which newspapers and websites advertise these types of jobs?
- Which agencies have TV companies on their books?
- What work experience do I need, and do I have it?
- If not, how can I get it?
- Do I know anyone who can help me?
- Is there any voluntary work I could do which would help?
- Is it worth sending my details to a company anyway, just in case?

Finally, losing weight; this is possibly the easiest to plan and the most difficult to achieve (I speak from personal experience!).

- What is your target weight?
- When do you want to achieve it? This time element is a vital part of any goal.
- How much must you lose each week?
- How will you achieve the weight loss (e.g. what will you eat, how much (specifically) will you exercise, etc.)

With all goals it's good to throw in an occasional treat for achieving targets on the way.

Establish a clear, specific plan, set yourself deadlines and stick to them. And, as Thomas Edison said, "Just when something seems impossible, that's the time to keep going." You can do anything.

**** Exercise ****

What are your goals?

Make them **CAN DO**

Goals should be something that you CAN DO they should follow this list:

Control - you have control over the outcome.

Achievable - you know it's something within your current skills and available resources or that you believe you can get the skills and resources required.

Necessary - you have a need to complete this objective. It will make life better.

Defined - the objective has clearly defined boundaries of what will be done and what won't be done. These must be precise so that you can say yes I've completed that.

On Schedule - the objective must have a time constraint that defines your schedule.

© Margaret Greenhall 2012

....
....
....
....
....
....
....
....
....
....
....
....
....
....

****

And finally, ...

Summary

At the beginning of this book, we reflected on how the role has changed substantially over the last 20 years or so, particularly the last 10 years. There is sometimes talk of Assistants being replaced by AI; these comments are only made by people who don't fully understand the modern role. AI will be an assistant for the Assistants; giving them more time to focus on the strategic and business elements of achieving the manager's objectives for the success of their organisation.

Learning to use the technology is the way forward but, most importantly, understanding the importance of relationship building, decision making and business acumen is what creates the Exceptional PA.

Do get in touch with your thoughts and comments ......

Good luck

Heather

Further Reading

The Book on Recruitment, Carole Fossey. 978-0986829383

Eat, Drink & Succeed, Laura Schwartz, 978-0615344539 (networking)

Lean In, Sheryl Sandberg, 978-0753541647 (gender equality)

Taking Control of your Inbox, Dr Monica Seeley, 978-1522708605

Conference & Event Management, Eth Lloyd, 978-0995700031

Change your Life with NLP, Lindsay Agness, 978-1620874264

The Executive Secretary Guide to Building a Powerful Personal Brand, Anel Martin, 978-1539535577

Suggestions for some of the exercises:

Page 21

What may make your tone of voice inappropriate?

Mood, health, priorities, confidence, assertiveness, embarrassment, who else is in the room or feeling defensive.

Page 27

Why do you think people see the negative side of things? Remember this is not just about you, it's also about your understanding of other people (emotional intelligence).

Past experiences, lack of confidence, ...

Page 28

Change these negative phrases into more positive statements.

1. "I'm having a terrible day."

Lots of challenges today; we'll get through them.

2. "That's going to be really difficult."

I'll get onto it straightaway as it'll take a while to achieve it.

3. "Why do they have to keep changing things?"

How will these changes benefit the organisation?

Page 35

1.   Unfortunately, priorities changed and the report will be finished by 2 pm.

2.   Excuse me, could I ask you a question?

3.   Excuse me, could I get a book from behind you?

4.   Would you like to sit here?

Page 39

Next time you have a tricky meeting, spend some time making sure you have all the background information about the topic and the person. What might you consider?

- The background to the topic,
- The other person's priorities, personality, temperament, pressures
- The impact of various decisions

Page 55

Write a note to three different people (one visual, one auditory and one kinaesthetic) to ask them to give you an idea of this month's sales figures:

1. We'd like to analyse the outlook for this quarter's sales. Could you give your view on the results for this month?

2. Could we have your remarks on this month's sales as we'd like to discuss the quarterly results?

3. We'd like to get a grasp of this quarter's sales. Could we have your feelings on this month's figures?

Page 56

Doesn't understand the filing system and too nervous to say
Doesn't understand what the documents are about
Didn't realise the urgency

Page 59

Do you feel you have failed at anything? If so, how could you turn this into a lesson learnt or even a positive? How can you now move on and not feel disillusioned?

Think about what went wrong and then consider what you have learnt from that and how it will help you in the future. For example, to take more time, to consider the wider impact of something, to double-check emails more carefully, to not be afraid of asking others ....

Remember, we are not robots, we will make mistakes. That is how we learn. It's our reactions to our errors that makes us professional.

Page 64

In your organisation specifically, what would a new person need to learn?

Organisation chart, dress code, interpersonal interactions, systems, history, corporate social responsibilities, mission statement, policies ......

Page 66

Jenny, who is very good at her job usually, has been showing some reluctance to attend meetings on behalf of her manager. Frances, the manager, is rather disappointed in her attitude.

When she speaks to Jenny, she learns that a previous unpleasant experience in a meeting, when someone ridiculed her suggestion, made her nervous about going again.

How could this be resolved?

Frances must convince Jenny that she has confidence in her abilities and that is why she is asking her to attend the meetings.

Remind her that the person who ridiculed her lacked emotional intelligence and she must remember she is the better person for not doing this sort of thing.

Remind Jenny that she has the choice of how to react. She can let the person hold her back or she can choose to move on – not easy but worth it.

Jenny should think of phrases she could use if anyone behaves in that way again. She probably won't need them but will take comfort from having them.

Page 75

What particularly motivates you?

Money, appreciation, learning, "fitting in", improving, success of the organisation, working in a team ...

What do you think motivates your manager and colleagues?

As above.

Page 77

Think of a situation where you may need a plan B.

Last minute decisions, others not fulfilling their commitments, weather, traffic issues, illness

What is your plan?

Your ideas

Turn these beliefs into empowering beliefs.

✗ **I've never been any good at ...**
✓ I've found this difficult in the past so I'm going to find a new way to ...

✗ **Nobody would take me seriously**
✓ I have good ideas and want to share them with other people and get their thoughts.

✗ **I'm not good enough**
✓ I am good enough

✗ **I can never do ...**
✓ I could do ...

✗ **I'm no good at ...**
✓ I could be good at ...

✗ **Everybody else is so much better/important/confident than me**
✓ Everybody else is different

✗ **Computers hate me**
✓ I am going to learn how to use computers

ISBN:
978-1532737602

How to Take Minutes of Meetings

I'd rather throw myself downstairs ....
That was how I used to feel about minute taking; this book is for those among you who feel the same. It is aimed at secretaries, PAs and administrators and covers the issues that worry them. These are the things that worried me and that have worried my hundreds of delegates over the last 15 years.

- ✓ Example minutes and agendas
- ✓ How to develop your skills in note taking
- ✓ Becoming more confident in your role
- ✓ A checklist of what to do before, during and after the meeting
- ✓ Help with layout and writing skills
- ✓ Learn what to include in minutes
- ✓ Understand how to become a better listener
- ✓ How to work well with your chairperson
- ✓ Lots of exercises and easy to read

ISBN:
978-1849370899

How to Write Excellent Reports

This book makes report writing a step by step process for you to follow every time you have a report to write. Margaret's understanding of how people read and remember gives a unique view of the process of report writing. This book brings you her tried and tested training techniques to make planning, writing and presenting a report straight forward.

"It's all about the reader."

- ✓ How to set objectives using 8 simple questions
- ✓ Exercises to help you enhance your skills
- ✓ Easy to follow flow chart
- ✓ Fun to use planning tools
- ✓ How to write an executive summary
- ✓ Types of reports and how to structure them
- ✓ How to layout the report
- ✓ Help people remember what they read

Lightning Source UK Ltd.
Milton Keynes UK
UKHW021609020320
359620UK00007B/506